# PRAIS
# YOUR LIGHT IS RISING

"In *Your Light is Rising*, Lisa McCrohan reveals her divine purpose: meeting human beings right where they are and gently offering them permission and tools to cultivate their pathway to peace. This book is a gift to its reader, and it goes beyond that; I see this as a gift to humanity. *Your Light is Rising* taps into the power of human resilience and the power of feeling seen. It is my greatest hope that the world will embrace this soul-soothing guide as a beloved companion for the most challenging moments of each day."

— Rachel Macy Stafford, NY Times bestselling author, speaker, and certified special education teacher, handsfreemama.com

"In a world of noisy should's and judgment, *Your Light is Rising* is so very, very different. Through her poetic wisdom, Lisa McCrohan outstretches her hand, reminds us to BREATHE, and lovingly invites us to both rest, and then move, within the strength, wisdom and grace of the 'Beloved.' Like a beautiful park in the middle of a loud, busy concrete city, *Your Light is Rising* serves as an oasis of peace gently inviting you to sit for a while upon an empty bench — admiring the green grass and the blooming flowers, listening to the birds chirp, and feeling the breath inside you flow more slowly, freely, deeply.

Then without warning, you're startled to hear the infectious laughter of children playing. And in that very moment, you remember who you are and who you were created to be. With one giant exhale — recharged and ready — you begin to move, to love, to create, to dance, to let your beautiful, one-of-a-kind-light

SHINE! And meanwhile, watching all of this unfold nearby is your dear friend, Lisa — her eyes smiling, her hands clapping as she joyfully cheers you forward each and every step of the way."

—Christy Lightfoot Berning, The Joy Movement

"Your Light is Rising nurtures my belief that my dreams and passions are possible. Lisa's poetry reminds me how close the Divine Spirit really is to us, always proud, always loving, always ready to smooth the path for us. This poetic guide is like a portal to unconditional beauty and love."

—Maria DiLorenzo, Personal Stylist, MFDStyle.com

"Lisa's words are truly balm for the soul. With her gentle presence and support through our everyday journeys, she moves us all with her poetry. Lisa is somehow able to create a safe space and haven for all the ups and downs we may be feeling. This is the type of book to leave bedside and read it over and over."

Tracy Brooks, Writer and Shamanic Practitioner, soulbeckons.com

"On the surface, Lisa McCrohan's latest work, Your Light is Rising, is filled with all of the things she is so, so good at offering us: hope and possibility, opportunities for awakening. Spend time sinking into the experience of her mission for us, and there is much more to discover. Lisa's guidance and promptings allowed me to release grief previously inaccessible, and to shed tension that was holding me away from people I love. There is not a greater gift than this. I'm imagining a world in which we all turn to Lisa's words in the moments of pause within our days (instead of to our phones — as Lisa suggested!). What a more authentic and resonant world it would be."

—Meghan Nathanson, Writer and Artist, meghannathanson.com

"Lisa's poetry is balm for our tired soul's right now. *Your Light is Rising* is filled with the life-giving fuel we need to rise up and keep living into our truths. This is my new morning inspiration to have by my side.

— Shawn Fink, Speaker and Life and Well-being Coach, shawnfink.com


"Such a beautiful gift! Lisa's warm embrace toward self and others within these pages is the soothing balm our weary souls need. *Your Light Is Rising* invites us to shine a soft light into our dark corners to help us heal our tender spots with compassion and kindness."

— Judy Bazis, Founder, Illuminate Festivals, illuminatefestivals.com


"Lisa gifts us a new way to see ourselves through the beauty and truth of poetry. Her hopeful words leave me feeling seen and inspired to reframe how I think about my day, my family's rhythms, and my connection to myself and my community. Our world would flourish if all mothers read this book and practiced the sacred pauses from *Your Light is Rising*. Lisa invites us to step away from the distractions of our modern world and into the sacred within us. Her poems are a calling – one well worth answering. I encourage you to read this compassion-filled book as a way to pause – truly taking time for yourself & making space for love."

— Lori Beth Auldridge, Host of The Elevating Motherhood Podcast, elevatingmotherhood.com

# YOUR LIGHT
## *is Rising*

### Kindling
### the Courage
### of Your Soul

# LISA MCCROHAN

Cover design by Pixelstudio.

Author photo by Sarah Burns Photography.

 Year of the Book
135 Glen Avenue
Glen Rock, PA 17327

ISBN 13: 978-1-64649-121-6
ISBN 10: 1-64649-121-1

Library of Congress Control Number: 2020918684

# Dedication

To my parents who have always supported and encouraged me to listen to the Divine Within and follow what delights my heart.

# Acknowledgments

Thanks to contributing editors Molly Spence and Demi Stevens.

My deep gratitude goes out to all the supporters of my Kickstarter campaign for their help in making this book a reality.

I would like to offer a special thank you to the following people for their generous support:

Mary Ann & Bob Ackerman

Judy Bazis

Christy Lightfoot Berning

Shannon Boros

Eleanor M. Breslin

Rosemary & Ted Brooks

Denise Castner

Julie Fasick-Johnson

Anthony & Nancy Holincheck

Cynthia Kennedy

Erin McKinney

Nicole Martino Mitchell

Gretchen Nonemaker

Colleen Crandall Parker

Neil Roed

Rachel Van Tassel

Bianca Maria Zago

Your belief in this project and your generosity are deeply appreciated.

# Contents

*Introduction*.................................................................. iii

## Dawn: Hope

Today is a New Day ................................................................3
The Invitation...........................................................................5
At the Start of the Day ........................................................7
With You......................................................................................9
Today .........................................................................................10
Hope ..........................................................................................11
Your Heart Will Be Satisfied ............................................14
Beside You ...............................................................................16
Hope Finds a Way.................................................................18
It's Possible .............................................................................21
Sacred Possibility ................................................................24
Nourished ...............................................................................25
Each Moment..........................................................................27
I Devote Myself Entirely to This Moment ....................28
Everyday Blessings..............................................................30

## Morning: Courage

Courage......................................................................................33
Rising..........................................................................................34
Your Wings................................................................................35
The God in You.......................................................................36
One Day She Realized ........................................................38

How You Rise........................................................40

What's Sacred ......................................................41

Two Empty Hands ...............................................43

No Longer Waiting...............................................45

It's Time to Begin ...............................................47

Answering the Wild Call......................................51

Take the Soul Risk...............................................54

Start Now..............................................................57

One True Voice to Follow ...................................60

Born to Shine ......................................................62

## Midday: Strength

Strength................................................................65

Gentle and Strong...............................................67

The Soul's Way ...................................................68

I Will Carry You...................................................70

Dropping the Armor ...........................................72

Unfolding .............................................................73

Flow .....................................................................75

A Promise to Myself ...........................................77

You Know Who You Are .....................................78

Don't Wait............................................................81

The Soul's Truth .................................................83

The Gospel Within You .......................................85

Wildly Herself......................................................87

Completely Free...................................................92

Truth.....................................................................96

## Afternoon: Compassion

Choosing Compassion ............................................................ 99
Tenderness............................................................................101
Self-Love...............................................................................102
Each Part...............................................................................103
Forgiveness............................................................................106
Mercy......................................................................................109
A Vow of Forgiveness ..........................................................110
The Inner World of Another Human Being....................112
Make Time for Love..............................................................113
Keeping Love Simple............................................................117
The Choice to Love...............................................................120
Loved as You Are ..................................................................122
Bath Time...............................................................................124
The Invitation to be Held ...................................................127
Go Gently................................................................................131

## Evening: Peace

It's Time for Quiet ................................................................137
Learning What is Good Enough..........................................139
Here All Along.......................................................................141
Sacred Softening ..................................................................142
Walking the Path of Beauty................................................144
Taking Refuge .......................................................................145
An Unbound Heart.................................................................146
The Poetry of Heaven ..........................................................147
When Only You Remain........................................................148
My One Desire........................................................................149
Whispers in the Silence........................................................151
A Woman's Peace in Mid-Life.............................................152

Moments .................................................................. 154
Silence .................................................................. 156
The Way Home .................................................... 157


Conclusion .............................................................. 161

# Introduction

## Soul Courage

There is a soul courage rising from within me
to clear out the distractions of daily life
and listen to my Inner Voice
calling me to surrender the old beliefs
that have kept me constantly questioning
my worth, ideas, and brilliance

and trust the truth I know in my bones:

I have a light to shine,
a wildness to embody,
and a medicine to share.

How bold! How audacious!
Yet, how true.

And it's time to shine,
time to remember the wildness within,
time to share this unapologetic, embodied pleasure
with others –

the pleasure of slowing down to hear the whispers of your heart,
the pleasure of moving your body in sensual, healing ways,
and the pleasure of channeling your light to shine in this world
that's hungry for your authentic wisdom, leadership, and art.

There is a holy desire rising from within us
to risk letting go of the life we have
and go on the wild adventures our souls want us to experience –
with healthier boundaries that protect our time,
honor our bodies, and breathe joy into our days.

This requires simple but sacred rituals in our day
that help us to pause, call back our attention
and place it on the altar of our hearts,

bowing to the wisdom of our bodies
to soothe our collective weariness with
time offline, outside, in nature, and with each other,

letting our hips shake to ancient rhythms that
our bodies intuitively remember,

creating art that speaks our truth
and reminds us of our belonging,

and offering our hands and hearts in service
in ways that do not deplete us,
but rather nourish us
and inspire others to live with bold authenticity
and compassion.

We have a light to shine,
a wildness to embody, and a medicine to share.

Come, take my hand.
Let's stand together at dawn
with our feet firmly rooted into the earth
and our hands on our hearts
tending to the temple of our bodies
as the light of hope begins to glow.

As we go into the morning,
let's call forth the soul courage within us
to stay true to what is sacred and
remember our divine essence
as we let go of what no longer serves our souls
and say "yes" to the next right step
in the direction of our dreams.

As the noon sun rises,
let's redefine strength as
dropping the armor around our hearts,
and softening the harshness,
allowing ourselves and others to be imperfect,
and still radiantly shining.

As the afternoon approaches and we might be edgy and tired,
let's love ourselves and others with tenderness and mercy,
remembering that we belong to one another
so that our homes may be a refuge for our dear ones,

our communities may be places of connection,
and our world may be united, more inclusive, and kinder.

As the sun sets and the moon rises,
let's end the day together with practices of surrender,
letting go of our worries
as we rest in the radiant Heart that leads us home.

There is a soul courage rising from within us
calling us to remember that
I – you – we matter.
Each of us has a light to shine,
a wildness to embody, and a medicine to share.
And it's time for us to rise. Together.

It's time to listen to the Divine within you and honor what you hear. It's time to answer the sacred call to live, love, lead, parent, and serve as your soul guides you. It's time to kindle your inner light, embodying the wildness within your soul, and share the medicine only you have with this world.

In our fast-paced, always-on modern world that's full of noisy distractions, listening to the voice of the soul isn't easy. We can often feel frazzled, lonely, overwhelmed, and disconnected from our hearts, bodies, one another, nature, and the Divine. In working with my psychotherapy and coaching clients, we call this "soul exhaustion." We long for authentic connection. We desire harmony to flow in our bodies, minds, and souls. We are hungry for true soul nourishment. We know – deep in our bones – that our souls have art to create, music to compose, movements to lead, and a light to shine – not only for our own personal wellbeing, but also for the world to be a kinder, more loving, and inclusive place. But how do we do that when life is so noisy, harsh, and distracting?

I wrote *Your Light is Rising* to be your poetic guide and journal to come back home to yourself through small, sacred pauses throughout your day that kindle the light of your soul to shine.

I love to and need to get up early in the morning, to pray, stretch my body in ways that honor my feminine form, write poetry, and journal my conversations with the Divine. To be honest, I often wake up anxious with my mind already running through the list of what's on the agenda for the day. Instead of trying to go "head to head" with my anxiety, I have to take that morning pause to get grounded and anchored – even for a few moments. This is how I stay sane and sense hope blossoming in my heart. In a world that will harshly push us to hurry, we can easily head off into our day without an anchor, toppled over by information, news, and other people's opinions and ideas. Our senses can get overwhelmed while our nervous systems become awash in anxiety and self-doubt. The Voice of the Beloved calling us to live with soul courage and let our light shine brightly can get drowned out.

No, I want to start my day sensing how the hand of the Divine holds me in the sea of this human experience. I want to start my day feeling the light of my heart glowing stronger as I listen for the ways the Beloved wants me to live with soul courage, washed with waves of holy aliveness that courses through me, with Love and Compassion as my soul fuel.

I love to and need to pause throughout my day – even just for a few moments – to clear out the distractions that pull on my precious attention. In midlife now, this is how I return home to myself and sense the Divine filling me up with soul courage to say "yes" to only the opportunities that spark joy in my soul rather than those "have to's" and "shoulds" that dim my light and that I listened to as a younger woman for too many years. It's how I practice dropping the mainstream definitions of strength that made me push myself too harshly and redefine strength as fierce devotion to inner gentleness – toward my body, ideas, dreams, and desires. It's how Grace opens me to compassion when I overreact, react out of fear, or get overwhelmed by the harshness of this world. It's how the light of my soul continues to break through the walls around my heart and shine – for my flourishment and for those I serve in my work and in my life.

I love to and need to end my day with quiet time. I could easily stay at my desk long after it is necessary, trying to perfect what I'm working on. But by putting into place healthy boundaries and having an evening ritual of quiet, I can sense the Divine calling me to put the work away and rest. It's how I can feel my light being replenished and nourished. It's how I can let go, forgive, and surrender.

The poems in *Your Light is Rising* were inspired by such moments with the hope that when you read them, you, too, may feel yourself being nourished – body and soul.

Divided by five key times of day, *Your Light is Rising* kindles the light within you throughout your waking hours: **Dawn** calls forth hope to blossom in your body and soul; **Morning** invites you to practice courage; **Midday** gently challenges you to redefine strength; **Afternoon** asks you to plant seeds of compassion in your own heart and in your relationships; and **Evening** readies you for sleep with soothing inspirational words of peace. After each poem, you'll find a short Kindling Your Light soulful reflection or embodiment practice as well as space to journal your responses, wonderings, or insights designed to help you connect to your body, your heart, and the wisdom within you.

This book is yours! Mark it up. Make it your journal. Write in it. Put post-it notes in it. Doodle in it. Keep it on your nightstand, kitchen table, or desk. Put it in your car so you'll have it for those times you are waiting and you usually reach for your phone – in a doctor's waiting room or at your child's sports practice – or bring it with you to read on your commute to work. Doodle your insights and inspirations in it. Carry it with you on a hike or sit on your porch and soak in a poem. Tear out a page to give to a friend. Read a poem aloud at the start of a staff meeting to settle coworkers' nervous systems and spark inspiration. Share a poem with a soulful group you are a part of and do the accompanying practice together, share your responses to the question, or journal on the reflection.

There are so many ways to read *Your Light is Rising!* You may choose to read it from cover to cover, reading one poem a day during your quiet reflection time. You may give yourself a short sacred pause, and briefly turn to a poem in the section that matches the time of day to breathe, reconnect to your body and heart, kindle your light, and feel re-inspired. You might make this your journal and write or doodle your responses and reflections. Perhaps when you feel ungrounded, scattered, or distracted in your day, you will whisper a prayer, "Please guide me" and randomly open to a page for an embodied soulful energy boost. Follow your intuition and let your heart guide you.

No matter how you read or share this book, *Your Light is Rising* is my way of encouraging and accompanying you.

You matter. You are worthy of love and rest. Your dreams matter. They are worthy of sacred attention and regard. You have a light to shine, a wildness to embody, and a medicine to share. May each of these poems and practices be like a spark within you, kindling your light, calling forth the courage of your soul to risk going on the adventures your soul wants to take, and inspiring you to share your light with the world. May our magnificent light shine and may we inspire a more compassionate, unified world.

I am alongside you. Please take my hand. Now, more than ever, we need each other. We are all in this together.

# Dawn

## Hope

## Today is a New Day

Today is a new day.

I begin this day
with my hand on my heart –

breathing in kindness,
breathing out kindness.
I choose to softly smile.

Relaxing my shoulders,
I know that God accompanies me
wherever I go.
I am loved –
deeply, tenderly, completely.

I let this love flow from me
as an offering to all those
I will greet today.

Today is a beautiful day.

Kindling Your Light Practice

Pause for a moment this morning. Feel your feet on the earth. Feel the support of what you are sitting on. Feel the integrity of your spine – the tailbone pointed down toward the earth and the crown of the head reaching up to the sky. Put your hand on your heart and feel yourself breathing in and out for a few breaths. With kindness and curiosity, what do you notice? In your body? In your heart? In your mind? You can use this space to write what you notice.

## The Invitation

There is a sacred moment
right now
when you awaken.
You open your eyes,
and you can answer "yes"
to the invitation of your soul
to be freely who you are,
as you are,
standing or dancing
in your power.
Because today,
today, you are honoring
your truest self.
You are answering the call
to live and speak and love
as your soul speaks to you.
And this is freedom.

Kindling Your Light Reflection

What does your soul want you to say "yes" to today?
Write it here.  Name it, announce it, claim it!

## At the Start of the Day

Kindle the light within you.
Let your breath become vibrant.
Stretch your body – reaching for the sky
and then bowing to the earth.
Let your movements slowly build strength
and generate heat.
Gently circle your neck and shoulders.
Swirl your hips, wrists, and ankles.
Soften the muscles in your face.
Lift from the back of your heart
up to the heavens.
Feel the light of your heart pulsing
stronger, more vibrantly.
Bow again to the earth.
Massage your whole body with
your loving hands.
Surrender to grace
and the light within you –
vowing to see the light in others.

## Kindling Your Light Practice

Move your body in ways that feel juicy and nourishing for three minutes. After you give yourself this mini sacred pause of embodiment, what do you notice? What has shifted – in your mind, emotions, mood, or body? Note how simple this is and how quickly you can shift your energy.

## With You

Maybe the Universe is asking you
to trust even more deeply
to surrender even more fully

to not know and still
take a leap into the darkness
and find that not only do you have wings
but a thousand angels and ancestors
are with you.

### Kindling Your Light Practice

Quiet yourself. Soften or close your eyes. Settle into your
body and breath. Then imagine who your angels and
ancestors are that support you, protect you, and guide
you. Bow to them. Thank them.

# Today

Today I vow to be kind with my words,
gentle with my touch,
and compassionate with my presence.

### Kindling Your Light Reflection

What vow will you make to yourself today? Put your hand on your heart and speak it into existence today.

## Hope

When there seems no other way
but through the darkness

when the light of hope flickers out

when you wonder how you will
make it through
or if you will ever be happy again –

please, take my hand.

I will lend you my hope.

I will bring you flowers
and I will empty the vase when they wilt,
and I will keep coming to visit
with flowers and a meal.

I will listen or just sit beside you
in silence
because there isn't anything to say.

We will breathe together
and ask for grace
that one day
the air will not feel so cold against your skin,
the empty space so lonely,
the night so long.

Hope will not be lost forever.
The Beloved will have the final say.
Grace will meet you where you are –
alone on the bathroom floor,
in a crowded subway station,
at the kitchen sink washing dishes,
or on a walk with a friend –
and then you will feel it:

Hope budding
after the harsh winter of grief
like a tenacious cherry blossom
on an early spring morning.

You will sense possibility
and hear a whisper from Beyond
that you will
be okay.

### Kindling Your Light Reflection

Who lends you hope? Whose hand reaches out to you when you are low on hope? To whom in your life could you lend hope?

## Your Heart Will Be Satisfied

I see your suffering.

I will not let that ache within you
remain forever tender and raw.
I will not let your cry go unheard.

I will satisfy your deepest longings.
I will soothe your anxiety.

I will not let you go cold and hungry.
I will not leave you to go about life alone.
I will find you wherever you are,
wrap a warm blanket around you,
make you tea,
and feed you soup and bread.

I will sit beside you until you gain your strength.
You will not be alone.
You will not walk through life wilted and hurting.

I will bring you into my arms and hold you.
I will call on the angels to guide you.
I will lend you my strength and hope.

The earth – with its flowing rivers and meadows,
mountains and forests –
will show you how to see beauty again.

Your body will know comfort and pleasure again.

Your heart will be satisfied.

### Kindling Your Light Practice

Take a moment and imagine a Divine Presence that wishes you such goodness, that wishes your soul to be satisfied. If this feels foreign to you, reimagine the Divine! So often the images of the Divine we have been taught do not resonate with the essence of our souls. Let your soul guide you in imagining a tender Presence with whom you can show up authentically and share your hungers, hurts, doubts, fears, and hopes. Start slowly or wildly! Use the words that resonate with you: Divine, Great Mother, Beloved, Universe, and so on.

# Beside You

I walk beside you.
No need to worry.
I am here with you, at your side.
You do not go alone.
When you breathe in, breathe in my peace.
Let it flow into every cell in your body,
softening what has been bracing for too long now.
When you breathe out, breathe out your worries to me.
Let me take them and unburden you.

I walk beside you.
I will wrap a shawl around your shoulders
when you shiver from cold or fear.
I will listen to what troubles you
and just be with you.
You are never alone.

I walk beside you.
It's okay to take off the armor around your heart
and feel the sunlight warming your skin,
to feel fresh air filling your lungs,
to remember you are good
and you are loved.

### Kindling Your Light Practice

Play with your imagination and visualize the Divine sitting beside you, listening with total presence and love for you, with all the time in the world. Play with having a conversation with the Divine. You can write such a dialogue here.

## Hope Finds a Way

There is so much in this world that could
turn you depressed, bitter, and apathetic.
Just three minutes of the daily news is enough
to lose hope.

And yet, every morning,
darkness fades and the sun rises.
Hope arrives – sometimes quietly
but always tenaciously.
Hope will keep nudging you,
"Watch this!"

And then an unexpected friend
reaches out to you.

A stranger smiles at you.

The cashier at the drive-through
tells you that the car ahead of you
just paid for your coffee
(and doughnut!).

You see an elderly couple
walking hand in hand,
and you imagine
the great love and humility
it must have taken to
face life's challenges
and still be each other's best friend.

At church, the child in front of you
in her dad's arms, resting on his shoulder,
keeps looking at you
half asleep, half awake,
and you notice the gentle way her dad's arms
safely and sweetly hold her.

That's when you sense it –
you soften.
Hope flows into the spaces within you
that were rigid and tense.
A light rekindles in your heart.

Hope smiles and says, "I've been here all along.
It's just difficult sometimes to find me in the muck.
But just keep looking for me."

There is goodness in this world.
Light will always cast out darkness
and Love will always have the final say.

Kindling Your Light Reflection

Imagine you are putting on Hope Glasses. Make it your practice today to look at the world through these lenses. What signs of hope do you see around you and in our world? Make a list of where you find and feel hope. Keep adding to this list so you can look back on it when you need the reminder of signs of hope. What happens in your body, energy, and heart when you put on your Hope Glasses?

## It's Possible

My Dear One,

It's possible to slowly open your heart
and love without holding back.

It's possible to find five minutes in your day for silence –
to take time out to care for yourself and to remember
what it's like to rest with a nourished soul.

It's possible to grieve and cry and fall apart...
and still be whole.

It's possible to open the curtains
and let the sunlight heal you –
to love again, feel again, dream again, and hope again.

It's possible to forgive
and sense how your experiences have softened you
and have given you a heart to see more tenderly
and feel more
compassionately.

It's possible to spend less time running around
and spend more time BEING with your dear ones
so you pause to see your child's goodness
and receive your partner's kindness.

It's possible to finally treat yourself as worthy
and deserving of kindness –
to softly cup your cheek in your hand and begin
to use gentle words with yourself such as,
"Sweetheart" and "My Love."

It's possible to follow your heart
and do what you really love –
to begin that dream –
yes, the one you've put off for so long now
and the one that I've been calling you to –
with my abundance and blessing paving your way.

It's possible to do less and rest when your body needs it –
to slow down, play, still get work done, and
live with a radical trust that
it's not YOU who has to make it all happen.

It's possible to remember that you are not alone –
that you are so deeply held and loved… always.

It's possible to live as though this very moment is a gift
given freely
for you to embrace, enjoy,
and let go
when it is time
with a heart full
of surrender.

Love,
The One Who Makes It Possible

Kindling Your Light Reflection

Today I will believe it is possible to:

## Sacred Possibility

May you open to Sacred Possibility.
May you let go of efforting.
May you remember that you are
not the god to make it all happen.
May you slow down
to allow the wisdom of your body and spirit
to dance with the Divine's grace that
brings you into sacred alignment
with what is holy and true to you.
May Sacred Possibility
begin to organically flow within you,
illuminating your inner vibrancy
so it shines in this world
that is longing for
such light.

### Kindling Your Light Reflection

What might be possible if you let go of "efforting" and
trusted that the Universe is on your side?

## Nourished

Trust that you are being guided.
Lean into this trust.
Remember that you are held.
Always.

You are Source
manifested in this form.
Tend to this form of yours!
Your body yearns for
attention and care –
not "someday"
but now.
Today.
There is time.
Trust that
all you are responsible for
will be okay
while you nourish you
so that you can hear
the whispers of Source
more clearly and trust
with deeper surrender.

Kindling Your Light Reflection

What pleasure might you fully enjoy in this moment?
Make a list of "mini pleasures" that are right here and
available to you in your everyday life.

## Each Moment

I am waking up each day and
I am choosing to live in a way that
honors my heart, body, and spirit.
I am choosing joy.
I am choosing to believe that
such a divine vastness is inside of me
and I can live from this space
moment by moment
in my everyday life.

Kindling Your Light Reflection

How can you choose joy in this moment right now?

## I Devote Myself Entirely
## to This Moment

I devote myself entirely to this moment:
the morning sun slowly dissolving the darkness,
the oak tree I see from my bedroom window
standing so still,
the cool morning breeze kissing my skin,
the touch of my old quilt
caressing the curves of my body.

I devote myself entirely to this moment:
the aches in my bones,
the worries in my mind,
the half-hopes in my heart,
as I sense the spaciousness of Grace
that holds it all.
And I abide there.

I devote myself entirely to this moment:
this breath and the next one, too;
nothing to change or shift,
only welcome, watch,
and let go.

## Kindling Your Light Practice

Pause for a moment and just be right here. Soften or close your eyes. Devote this moment to just feeling yourself breathe – in and out. What do you notice when you bring a sense of devotion and reverence to this moment?

## Everyday Blessings

There are blessings all around me.
I open my eyes to see them.
I open my heart to welcome them.
I open my hands to share them.

### Kindling Your Light Reflection

Name three blessings in your life right now, and then
notice what happens in your body.

# Morning

## Courage

## Courage

Someday, you will look back at
this very spot where you stand now
as holy ground.
It will be the place where you finally stood still
and decided that you could not keep ignoring
the Voice Within You.
And though you weren't feeling brave
or completely certain,
there came this moment, at this exact spot,
when you felt yourself surrender everything
to the Beloved within you.

"Take me," you said,
"I'm Yours."

### Kindling Your Light Reflection

What has the Voice Within You been trying to tell you
lately?

# Rising

You were made for something bigger, bolder
yet softer and slower.

It's time to pause and listen within,
to move your body in ways that invigorate you
and embolden your feminine form.

You were meant for something freer, lighter,
and less harsh.

It's time to let go of what no longer serves you
and rise.

## Kindling Your Light Reflection

What is one habit or belief that can you let go of in your
life that no longer serves you?

## Your Wings

Why are you still playing small?
Rise up, my Love.
The nest you are in
is too small for you.
Jump out!
Take a leap
and fly!
You were meant to soar.
Your wings were meant to
draw people's eyes up
to the heavens
in awe.

### Kindling Your Light Reflection

How have you been playing small? What leap are you
being called to take right now?

# The God in You

What do you really want?
When you dig down deep,
when you are day-dreaming or
it's late at night and all is quiet.
What do you really want to be about?

Most of us don't give ourselves the time
and space to listen, discern, and then take action.
The God in You is waiting – wanting –
for you to listen and trust.

Maybe you don't know where to start.
Start with going for a walk.
Start with going to bed earlier.
Tune out what others are doing,
and tune into your heart.

Rumi had it right –
following what you love
will not lead you astray.

It's time to risk a big pause
and listen.

Kindling Your Light Reflection

What I really want is:

## One Day She Realized

One day she realized that
the person she needed to tend to the most
was her own self.
As a mother, a lover, a healer, a friend,
she understood that where she needed to
put her attention – every single day –
was on her own self-care.

So she decided to take charge of
her schedule, her time, and her energy
and let the world think what it wanted to.
For she knew that by deeply nourishing her own self,
she would teach her children how to do the same,
she would start a
revolution of radical self-honoring
with her soul sisters,
she would embody her power
and ask very clearly for what she needed –
at home, in her relationships, and in her work.
And she would be a powerful source of
healing for this world because of her
radical commitment to
self-compassion.

Kindling Your Light Reflection

What does radical self-responsibility look like in this season of your life?

## How You Rise

Your precious energy is wasted
in constant self-correction
and doubt.
Gather back all that energy
and put it into trusting
your brilliance
and sacred inner voice.

### Kindling Your Light Question

Make two lists: What do you waste your energy on and
where do you want to invest your energy?

## What's Sacred

What's sacred to you?
Yes, sacred.
Because that's what matters.
That's what you want to build your
life around.

"Sacred" means more than
"important."
Sacred goes soul deep.

How you love
in this human form
in your daily life
is the expression of
your soul's reason for being here.

Get clear about that.
Don't just wander.
Don't just aimlessly go about life.
You'll get pulled into the abyss of
what everyone else wants and
what the world thinks you should be and do.

There are way too many shiny objects
and distractions in our modern life.
In order to hear Your God talking to you,
you must step out of the noise
every day, for even just ten minutes.

Put your hand on your heart,
feel the breath moving in you,
feel the life force flowing through you.

Here your next steps will be guided.
You will embody and shine the light within you –
for your deepest wellbeing
and for the world to become a better,
more peaceful
and compassionate place
because of your clear devotion
to what's sacred.

Kindling Your Light Reflection

What is sacred to you?

## Two Empty Hands

I am standing with two empty hands
admitting that what WAS
is no longer working and
I am DONE turning my
attention to it.

I am open and empty.

I am opening the door to
welcome in new energy,
new possibility,
and new life.

I will not pick up just any old
thing and put it into these precious
hands of mine.

They will remain empty,
trusting, waiting.

I'll say "no" to old habits that
want to pull me back to
my old life like a
rubber band stretches but
returns to its known shape.

I'll go outside and walk in the woods.
I'll bake bread and make soup.
I'll wrap a blanket around me
and sit by the fire.
I'll remain steadfast, trusting,
and listening for the
holy YES
to rise from within me
that will guide my hands
to embrace what
must come next.

Kindling Your Light Practice

Stand on the earth, eyes closed, face to the sun, and palms
open, ready to receive.

## No Longer Waiting

When you are so done with
waiting for change
just to happen,
you finally realize that
YOU are the change.

Instead of waiting for
anyone else to do something
differently, instead of
playing victim,
instead of waiting to be
rescued,

you decide
it's about damn time for
you to rise.

So you rise and
you begin.
One foot
in front of the other.
One inhale, one exhale
at a time.

Old beliefs try to call you back
to your old ways.
But you are no longer listening.
You will not wait
any longer for change just
to happen.

You decide to BE the change
you were always waiting for.

Kindling Your Light Practice

Go from "I can't" to "I can" by focusing on what action you can take, what shift you can make, or what change you can lead.

## It's Time to Begin

There comes a time when you know
you must just begin.
And though you may be
caught in old habits that
leave you treading water
in half-hopes –

you trust.

You trust that what you desire
has been placed on your heart
by the Beloved and is therefore
a holy call to life.

And you decide to
finally give yourself
permission
to focus on
your creativity.

So you put down the
bag of cookies and
pick up the running shoes.

You write the words
you've longed to say
and you send the letter.

You clear off the kitchen table
and get out the paintbrushes
and watercolors.

You sit down at the desk
and type the words,
"Chapter One."

You dust off the guitar
and start singing.

You walk into the family room
where your dear ones
are reading or playing a
video game, and announce,
"I'm doing this.
Please support me."

With your hair pulled back,
sweat on your brow,
aging hands,
sagging breasts,
thighs that touch,
wrinkles on your face,
and doubts in your heart,
you begin.

Filled with stubborn focus
or fierce devotion,
you begin.

You know "hard."
And this isn't it.

Hard was speaking the
truth that your marriage
needed serious attention.

Hard was burying
your mom.

Hard was putting down
the bottle.

Hard was going through
another miscarriage.

Hard was cancer.

Those experiences now
fuel your steadfast devotion.
You know how to
let your thoughts just be
while you persevere.
It's time now.
And you know it.

"Alleluia!" you cry out
with paint on your hands
and a smile on your face.
"It's so damn time!"

Kindling Your Light Reflection

What is it so damn time for?

## Answering the Wild Call
## Within Her That Will Save Us All

There comes a time in a woman's life
when her body won't be tamed,
won't lie down and play nice,
won't be appropriate and good,
or won't sit and be still

when her body wants to move and tantalize,
to dance to the ancient drums of hearts beating –
calling to her,
to dance, sway, and moan –
to make the sounds that the world would squelch
and has been trying to keep down,
quiet, and dutifully still.

There comes a time in a woman's life
when she taps into her wild, untamed, sensual,
powerfully feminine self-expression
that scares a world that wants her to be
apologetically appropriate.
And it may scare her, too, at first
because she will be called many names.

Yet she is beyond that now,
responding to a deeper truth.
Her feminine form knows the deep waters of emotions.
She flows in harmony with the elements.
She intimately remembers the earth from which she came
and the clay used to make her form.

She knows that familiar wild call within
to rise,
unbound, unapologetic,
to sweat and dance,
move and make love

to herself,
her lover,
this world.

There comes a time in a woman's life
when she hears the familiar drumbeats –
her heartbeat pulsing with the Divine's –
and her body knows what to do.
She hears the wild music,
the call within,
to embody her destiny
that will surely save her.

Because she knows now that her own dance and poetry,
her swaying and speaking, praying and praising,
will call every woman to rise and remember her own path

to respond to the wild call within her heart begging her
to sweat and dance, move and embody her destiny
that will ignite the flames of change
and save
us all.

### Kindling Your Light Practice

Let the Self-Critic rest while you organically move your body and play with making sounds – any sounds! You might feel self-conscious at first, but as you allow yourself to play, notice how this feels liberating and even fun. What do you experience when you trust your body to move freely and to make the sounds it wants to make?

# Take the Soul Risk

Every day, we have the choice:
will we play it safe and keep going along
doing the things we have been doing,
or will we take a risk
to do something different?
Will we lean into our dreams
or pull back from how uncomfortable
it feels to take a chance?

Sure, it might not work out.
Your idea might fail.
You might look like a fool
or fall on your face.

But maybe it doesn't matter.
Maybe what matters is
taking the soul risk.
Maybe what matters is
going for your dream,
reaching out, taking a chance.

We want life to be comfortable and easy.
It's not.

Life is messy with no guarantees.
The world might appear harsh
and "against you" at times.

But your soul calls to you –
to write the novel that
might not be a best seller,
to hold out your hand
to a person who may not take it,
to paint the canvas that might not sell,
to start the project that no one may get behind.

But to not do it would mean
a part of you dies.
And so you have to take the soul risk
and feel uncomfortable.
You have to listen to your soul
because you refuse to
play it safe and easy.
You refuse to get to the
end of your life and
wish you would have.

You begin to learn that
bravery isn't the absence of fear.
It's being afraid AND
doing what you have to do.

Courage isn't something you muster up.
It's something that grows stronger within you
as you take that soul risk.

So begin.
Take the risk.
Be uncomfortable.
Reach out.
Go for your dream.

You will sense that
beneath the ebb and flow of
success or failure,
a deeper peace settles
in your soul.

And that is enough
to make taking the risk
worth it.

Kindling Your Light Reflection

What soul risk must you to take?

## Start Now

Start now.
Whatever it is that has
been on your heart
to try, create, or embrace –
take one soulful action today
toward that desire.

Life is so short and precious.
Let's live it with a full, imperfect,
messy, will-risk-love
heart.

We really do have the power
to change!

Even if you are carrying the
heavy weight of doubt and guilt,
even if you have tried several times,
even if you lost your hope
somewhere back a long while ago,
please know that there are
forces in the Universe that
want your heart to be
satisfied!

There are angels who are
around you, guiding you.
The Universe is filled with
benevolence.
I know it may not appear
that way at times.
I know it wears on a heart to
reach out once again.

So, dear one, let your tears
be prayer enough.
Let your open palms
be that one soulful action
emptying out of all grasping
so you can receive
another hand in yours,
a gift,
or a new song in your heart.

Start now
in any new moment.
The hand is here.
The gift is here.
The new song is already
playing sweet,
soothing lines
to rekindle
the creativity,
hope,
and love
in your heart.

### Kindling Your Light Reflection

What do you need to start right now? What is one soulful action you can take today to honor that soul need?

# The One True Voice to Follow

There comes a moment when you know

you must take that courageous leap out into the unknown –
to make that big move or drastic change,
to gamble everything
for the love growing within you.

Because it actually doesn't matter anymore
how the world responds
or even if you are right or wrong.

There is a new boldness and strength
in your steps now.
You are listening only
to how the
God Within You responds.
And what you hear –
loud and clear
over the rapid beating of your heart
and the voices of doubt swirling in your head
that were never yours to begin with –

is YES.

A deep, radical, life-altering,
aligning-my-feet-with-my-soul's-purpose

YES.

And so you and the God Within You

leap

hand in hand.

This is the moment you know
you were born to be this free.

### Kindling Your Light Practice

Take time today to visualize yourself aligning your life
with the YES from your soul.

## Born to Shine

You were born to shine
and offer this world your light,
a light that only YOU have,
a light that can heal this world
begging to be nourished with
your presence, your gift.
No one like you has ever been born
or will be created again.
It's your light the world needs.
Dear Heart,
now is the time to be bold,
speak that courageous "yes"
and embody what you have
been born to do.

### Kindling Your Light Reflection

What light do you have within you that needs to shine in
this world?

# Midday

## Strength

## Strength

True strength is not going through life with gloves on
and armor around your heart.
It's softening and saying things like,
"I'm sorry" and "I love you."

It's not "pulling yourself up by your bootstraps"
and going it alone.
It's allowing others see you when you are a mess
and letting them love you as you are.

It's not pushing through the grief and "carrying on."
It's making the sounds your grief has longed to make
that aren't pretty, planned out, or perfect.

True strength is not motivating yourself with harshness.
It's honoring yourself with kindness and regard.

It's not ignoring "what is" –
the marital challenge, the disappointment,
the diagnosis, the struggle at work.
It's pausing and admitting what is here.

It's not denying your emotions.
It's getting to know your fear, anger,
sadness, shame, and desire,
and treating each one with compassion.

True strength is not conquering your body.
It's befriending it.

It's not constantly correcting yourself.
It's learning to treat yourself with
tenderness and gentleness.

It's not achieving and succeeding.
It's fumbling, failing, and surrendering
to a Force greater than your willpower.

True strength is not going along with the crowd.
It's listening to your Soul and being the light
you were born to be.

Kindling Your Light Reflection

How do you define strength?

## Gentle and Strong

Start with purifying your body.
It doesn't have to be through rigid or harsh means.
Let it be motivated by love
and a desire to listen to your Source more clearly,
to make decisions and take actions
that are aligned with the Divine,
and to love yourself
so that your light radiates out into this world as
blessings all around you.

### Kindling Your Light Reflection

What is one way you can be gentle with your body?

# The Soul's Way

You think that you can control what will come
by planning and striving,
reaching and being ever so organized.
When you have "everything in place,"
you have the illusion of control.
For a while, you may feel satisfied,
the hunger seems quelled,
and all is quiet and neatly arranged.

But yet I call you into the unknown,
and ask you to not have it all planned out;
just hear my voice and leap into the mystery.
I have plans for you that you cannot
organize or plot out with colorful markers,
progressive steps, or a linear timeline.

This is not my way.
It is not the way to true freedom.
Freedom is here, right now,
surrendering, trusting,
believing in the possibility that
I can delight your soul
more than any planning
could ever offer you.

## Kindling Your Light Reflection

How do you try to control things in life? What suffering does this create? Forgive yourself for being human! Imagine the Great Mother blessing you and showing you how surrendering will strengthen you. Feel the freedom and ease. What does working and living in this way look like?

## I Will Carry You:
## A Promise from the Divine

You are not alone.
You are held, watched over, loved.
I will guide you through this.
You can let go of anything that
makes you feel like you don't deserve
happiness, abundance, and love.

You are mine.
I won't let you forget that.

Forgive yourself.
Forgive yourself.

Let go of the heavy burdens you carry.

You have light to shine and delight to share.
Let's not waste any more time being weighed down.

I am beside you.
It's time to lay it all down, Dear Heart.

I will carry you.

### Kindling Your Light Reflection

What can you lay down so you can rise up with a deeper inner strength? Even if you don't believe you deserve happiness, abundance, and love, what would happen if you just started acting like you did?!

## Dropping the Armor

One day –
maybe because it's time
or because the weight has become too crushing –
you drop the armor around your heart
so you can breathe
and love in this world
undefended.

### Kindling Your Light Practice

Give yourself a five-minute break and visualize yourself dropping the armor around your heart – slowly, piece by piece.

## Unfolding

Let it all unfold
as it is to be.

Wait.
Be still.

Just do the next right thing
that rises from your heart as the mud settles
and the water becomes
clear.

It is all unfolding
as it needs to be
for the world to receive
your presence.

Just let it unfold
with ease and breath
while resting
in the ancient arms
of spaciousness.

Kindling Your Light Reflection

Name something that you have wanted but isn't here yet. Notice how you have been relating to this desire. Do you struggle, work at it, or strive for it? What would it look like and feel like to trust, to just do the next right thing, and focus on what delights your heart? What spaciousness and ease arise?

# Flow

One day I decided that
I didn't want to be angry anymore,

I didn't want to hold onto the past,
I didn't want to keep nailing myself
to the cross or blaming others,
and I didn't want to keep
cutting myself off
from Love flowing in me, through me,
and between me and others.

I decided to forgive – myself and others –
out loud and whispered to my heart
again and again and again
in moments when
the old ways of thinking and relating
would try to drag me back.

I decided to have better boundaries
and care for myself as if I loved myself.

And slowly,
I learned that Grace shows up
when we open the door to our heart
just a crack,
and Light begins to pour into
the dark places within us
that have almost withered.
Almost.

Parched, these very spaces where
anger once raged,
Love begins to flow,
Gratitude begins to grow roots,
and Joy begins to blossom.

Kindling Your Light Practice

Notice when you are "in the flow" today and how that is
a deep, soothing, full-of-ease type of strength.

# A Promise to Myself

I hold myself in a way that is dignified and fierce.
I let go of what others will think.
I let go of making myself smaller
so others feel comfortable.
I speak my truth with wisdom.
I rise with light and compassion.

## Kindling Your Light Practice

Make a promise to yourself today. Write it here. Then stand in front of a mirror and speak your promise. Take your hands and let them move organically and bless your body with this promise. Then go into your day holding yourself in a way that is dignified and fierce.

## You Know Who You Are

It's time for you to rise.

It's time to get up and
honor your truth

live your dream

speak from your heart

and announce how it's going down.

You are done saying you are fine.

You are done playing small and
hiding your light.

You are done caring if you are
too shy
too loud
too fat
too skinny
too emotional
too intellectual
too you.

You are daring to drop the
"not enough" belief –
not talented enough
experienced enough
hip enough
pretty enough
smart enough
ready enough
confident enough –
that has kept your light
from shining.

You know who you are.
And the desire to accept yourself
as you are
has grown so strong that
now you are willing to risk
falling, failing, or looking like a fool.

You are willing to risk being
the leader of your own life
and allowing the fullness of
who you are
to rise, roar, shine,
and inspire others
to do the same.

Kindling Your Light Reflection

What risk would you take if you were 10% braver? How would you rise, roar, and shine? Imagine how this might inspire others to live with and embody such freedom and authenticity.

## Don't Wait

Don't wait
until you feel like you are
worthy or good enough
to treat yourself with
kindness and compassion

to go for your dreams

to pause working so hard
and stretch and
enjoy a cup of tea
and a quiet moment

to speak to yourself as you would
to your best friend

to touch yourself with gentleness

to wrap yourself in softness

to surround yourself with people
who regard you and love you
as you are

to truly nourish yourself

to expect miracles and
abundance
and deep love in your life.

Don't wait
until you feel like you are
worthy or good enough for love.

Just start acting like you are.

Kindling Your Light Practice

Just start acting like you are worthy and you are enough.

## The Soul's Truth

There comes a time when you just have to go for it,

when you know the deep truth within you
and you follow it.

Whether you totally fall on your face or
stumble over your words,
the plan isn't perfect,
you just have to do it

because anything else would be
death to your soul.

And there's a light now that you know

and it burns deep within you
and it's growing stronger, brighter.
It can't stay contained in you any longer.
It wasn't born to stay.

There comes a time when you just have to go for it

hands trembling, heart pounding,
light illuminating your whole body
reaching out into this world
with magnificence.

Kindling Your Light Reflection

Even if I fumble, stumble or fail, I just have to go for this:

## The Gospel Within You

There is a gospel within you that wants to be preached
with words – possibly – but mostly with your body

truth spoken through the way your feet stand firmly
and confidently on the earth

the way you
*t a k e*
*u p*
*s p a c e*

the way you are done caring about perfection or pleasing

the way you move freely – liberated from the religions
that have kept your hips,
breasts, and lips bound, expressionless, and quiet

the way your eyes reveal the unshakable truth you
know deep in your bones
that you – we – are Her.

Kindling Your Light Reflection

What's the gospel within you that has to be preached?

## Wildly Herself

One day she decided
that it was more important to love
than to be right.

She knew that she had a choice:
she could remain closed off,
hold back her love, and be angry and bitter.

Or she could love
and create room for herself, her partner,
her children, and her parents to be human.

But she was pissed. And she knew she was right!

And yet, lying there on the cold, hard floor,
she was done working so hard
to prove how right she was.

Looking at her reflection,
she saw the bitterness.
She couldn't remember the last time
she truly laughed.
She wanted her life back.
She wanted joy to flow through her again.

She stood there staring at her clenched fists.

Then she leaned back, closed her eyes,
opened her hands,

and decided to love –

first

herself.

This, of course, meant taking back her power.
It meant no longer blaming and waiting to be rescued.
This meant facing her fears of speaking her truth,
being rejected, being told she wasn't enough,
being told she was too much,
and ending up alone.

She decided not to conquer her fears with harshness,
but rather to embrace them with tenderness.

At first such vulnerability felt like brokenness.

She cried. She felt needy. She felt weak.

Yet, slowly, gradually,
her attention shifted from the outside,
and rested inside
at the temple of her heart.

Her devotion to inner gentleness
poured light into her wounds.

As she softened,
she came to know her true strength.
And as she began to let herself be human,
she began to love her whole body
with gentle caresses, nourishing food,
sunlight, and air.
She began to let the river of her emotions flow
and trust the wisdom of her body.

She began to bring her desires into the light,
and admit her true passions.
She began to take one step each day
to honor those desires –
which looked a lot like love
and felt a lot like truth.

And every day, this fierce devotion to loving herself
gave way to a wild freedom within her.

She stopped waiting for someone else
to bring her flowers.

She stopped taking responsibility for
everyone else's happiness.

She stopped asking for the world to see how right she was.

She stopped asking for permission or anyone's opinion.
And she started being honest with what she needed
and even with what she secretly desired.

She started making the sounds her body needed to make
even though this made people feel uncomfortable.
They wondered if she was "going crazy"
and if it was "her time of the month."
Some put a hand on hers and told her to calm down.
Which, of course, she wouldn't.
Not this time.

And for the first time
since she was a little girl standing outside
feeling the cool morning air on her skin,
the cells in her body tasted freedom.

Such embodied self-love and reverence
started to dismantle decades of beliefs
her culture and church had placed on her
and she had carried for too long now.

She began to feel so free
that the desire to be right dissolved
like salt in warm water –
holy water –
poured over her divine body
as sweet forgiveness

self-forgiveness

for every time she had abandoned herself
in order to please someone else.

Wildly herself,
Love coursed through her
like warm lava slowly rising –

as if earth, fire, and air were meeting
in the vast ocean of her heart
where boldness, truth, and compassion
flowed endlessly in and through
her holy body.

And she discovered that
her heart had been right all along –
the kind of "right" that feels like
real love
for herself
and this world.

Kindling Your Light Reflection

Will you be bitter or have better boundaries to be fiercely
devoted to loving yourself?

## Completely Free

I am barefoot now, feeling the grass between my toes,
the warm sun against my shoulders.

I watch my daughter snap on her helmet with little hands
that seem much older than a week ago,
and get onto her scooter.

My son zips by me on his big-boy bike.
"Mom, do you see me?!" he asks,
eyes bright, alive.

I feel my heart suddenly arrive right here,
my breath drawing my attention to this
precious, fleeting moment.

I am quiet

noticing the little curls sticking out from under her helmet,
his strong legs – how they so seamlessly pedal faster and faster,
the light in his adventurous eyes,
the angelic way she calls me
"Mommy."

"This is holy," I say to myself. "This is what matters."

Moments ago I was lost
trying to get too much done, too quickly.
There are dishes to wash, deadlines to meet,
worries that keep me tense and my belly in knots,
and regrets that flood my mind late at night when all is quiet.

But today,
I choose to stay right here.
And as I do, the aching truth of this "holy now" fills my heart.
I could fall to my knees and kiss the ground
with my whole body grieving and letting go,
while my lips can only whisper,
"Thank you."

Breathing in blessing, breathing out blessing. This is prayer –
prayer as deep as sitting in silence on retreat
wrapped in my prayer shawl.
Now the "everyday" is my church, my meditation cushion.
My children and my beloved are my prayer shawl,
drawing me into the very space within my heart
where I touch Home.

I want to notice these gems in my everyday life
amidst the mess and imperfect.
I want to let go of anything
that keeps me from embracing my life and this world
with a delight-filled heart.

I want to arrive right here –
in this holy now –
fully present, awake, gentle,
pushing nothing away,
allowing "what is"
to free my soul.

Hafiz was right:
*"One regret, dear world,*
*that I am not willing to have*
*when I am lying on my deathbed*
*is that I did not kiss you enough."*

It is delighting in this very moment
that nourishes my soul
tethering me to,
reminding me of,
who I am.

This is my path:
to walk, to notice,
to wake up in such a way
that I am so aligned
with the one prayer of my Heart –
to be and embody Delight.

All these years, searching for
wholeness, rest, and happiness
only to arrive right here
in this very moment

completely free.

### Kindling Your Light Reflection

What's the one regret you are not willing to have when you are lying on your deathbed? List all the micro actions and soul risks you can take to live without regret in your everyday life.

# Truth

To be tender and gentle
is power.

To give without expectation of
return or recognition
is service.

To love without holding back
is freedom.

## Kindling Your Light Reflection

What are your own definitions of power, service, and
freedom?

# Afternoon

## Compassion

## Choosing Compassion

Every single time
we choose compassion
over hardening our hearts
and pulling away,
we find that the fear within us
actually begins to dissipate.

The hurt within us
begins to heal.
We find that being tender
and "choosing connection"
feels a lot more like home...
and freedom.

We let go of old beliefs that
kept us separated.
We let go of old ways of
treating ourselves and others
that kept us living half alive.

Instead, we find it refreshing
to choose compassion
because it becomes our
only truth to remembering
why we are all here.

Kindling Your Light Reflection

Pause and reflect on a situation where you normally get triggered. What is happening in your body, mind, and heart? How could you choose compassion for yourself and others in this situation?

## Tenderness

Tenderness
rekindles the
light of your
heart.

### Kindling Your Light Practice

Say a dear one's name tenderly and kindly today.

## Self-Love

Maybe you don't have to do so much,
try so hard, expend so much energy
trying to keep everything together.
Maybe you are carrying too much –
much more than is humanly possible.

Maybe it's time to go easy on yourself –
to be gentle, to soften the harshness,
and to talk to yourself like you would
a dear friend who needs compassion.

Maybe it's time to let yourself feel the
pleasure of slowing down, doing less,
and finally choosing to love yourself.

### Kindling Your Light Practice

As you go about your day, ask yourself, "How can I soften
in this moment?

# Each Part

Can you meet
each part of yourself –

the pleasant one,
the rowdy one,
the shameful one,
the bullying one,
the fake and pretending one,
the wounded one,
the brilliant one,
the wise one –

as an old friend

welcoming each one as a
sacred aspect of yourself?

Can you treat each one with
kindness, offering them tea
or space to rest, talk, dance,
be quiet, or be held?

They don't need fixing
or lecturing,
but rather
loving presence.

Putting the bully in isolation
doesn't heal.
Lecturing the anxious one
doesn't work.
Toughening up the wounded one
doesn't make you stronger.

It's time for a radical way of healing
with inclusion and loving presence.

"I see you are hurting,"
softens the bully.

"I see you are afraid,"
calms the anxious one.

"I see you have been through a lot,"
acknowledges the one who has tried
to be the world's version of strong
for too long now.

Each part is here
to bring you back home to yourself.
Each part expresses a desire
for Love.
For union.
For wholeness.

### Kindling Your Light Reflection

Instead of treating certain parts of yourself with harshness, learn to "tend and befriend" each part by saying to it, "I see you and I care about what you need to feel safe." Journal with one part of yourself that you have neglected or treated harshly. Let this part know that you want to "tend and befriend" it.

## Forgiveness

You've held onto this, carried it for so long
that your shoulders have rounded,
caved in around your heart.

Slumped over,
protecting this wounded place,
you have been taking half breaths –
short and shallow –
for years now.

My Dear,
maybe it's time.

Maybe it's time to come
and sit here beside me.

We have all the time in the world.
I am ready to listen.
Please come.

You don't need to rush or worry about me.
I am here just to be alongside you.

Take up space.

In the words and the silence,
in the cries and the trembling,
I am here.

Slowly,

in such spaciousness,
candlelight gently unveils
the regrets and sorrows
rising from the base of your belly
beating against your ribs.

Slowly,

you touch the grace
that has been here all along
holding you.

You breathe into spaces now open
that have been squeezed tight
longing for air.

Raw. Tender.
Yet alive.
So very alive.

It's impossible now to stay closed, armored.

Rest embraces you,
forgiveness flows effortlessly
in you
and from you.

You know your true home when you feel it
and all that remains now

is Love.

～

Kindling Your Light Practice

Take a moment and imagine sitting with the Great Mother. Whatever regrets you have been holding onto, imagine sharing what you have been carrying. What's it like to share these? Open to the Great Mother's love for you. Imagine her love flowing into you like sunlight for your whole body and soul.

## Mercy

I could have
shown my love
more
to you.
But I was afraid
that I would
explode into
a million pieces.

Please forgive me.

### Kindling Your Light Reflection

How can you show mercy to someone today?

# A Vow of Forgiveness

When I feel the desire to be unkind,
to judge harshly, to pull away,
or to blame,

I vow to wake up in that moment and
remember that all of us want to be loved,
to be touched, to belong,
to know we are good, and to be seen.

I vow to pause,
put my hand on my heart, and
say, "Please forgive me" –
to my own heart first and then to others.

I vow to love all the parts of me
that I tend to treat not so kindly.

I vow to extend kindness and regard
to all those I meet – stranger or dear one.

I vow to go gently, to soften, and
to be fiercely devoted to kindness, love,
compassion, and delight.

This includes caring for myself
and having the wisdom to discern
that sometimes the kindest act
is to love ourselves and others so fully
that we let go.

I vow to forgive –
letting go
letting go
letting go

so only love remains.

## Kindling Your Light Practice

What is your own vow of forgiveness? (It can be short!)
Repeat it silently to yourself whenever you are triggered
so that you can more quickly let go and live with clearer
energy and love – for yourself and others.

# The Inner World
# of Another Human Being

The truth is that
we don't know the inner world
of another human being.
We don't know their particular
story, grief, or pain.
We tend to take it personally,
when really, they are just
trying to get through the day.

Instead of a critique, a harsh look,
or a defensive posture,
offer a blessing.
Extend compassion.
Give space for others
to be imperfect.

## Kindling Your Light Practice

Practice taking things less personally today.

## Make Time for Love

Make time for love in your day
amidst the hurry,
tackling the "to do" list,
always waiting for a pause
to do what really matters,
but every night falling into bed
exhausted, saying,
"I'll do it tomorrow."

Make time for love when you wake up.
Gently stretch, breathe in the blessings
in this very moment
and ask yourself,
"How do I want to live today?"

Make time for love in your morning
before you put on your shoes and you are out the door
to hold your child – two-year-old or teen –
with a look that says "I am your biggest fan."

Make time for love at lunchtime
to slowly eat and taste your food
to find some gem
as you talk to your coworker,
fix a sandwich with your child,
or sit with your aging parent
and wipe crumbs from the corner of their mouth.

Make time for love in your afternoon
to put down your cell phone
to turn toward your child
and tell him how you longed for him
before he was born,
how you think she is a lovely human,
just as she is.

Make time for love in your evening
to see your husband and how he wants you to be happy
to see your wife and how much she holds.
To say, "I see you, my Love."

Make time for love before bedtime
to finally tend to what your heart holds
and give yourself space to breathe,
to say thank you, forgive, and let go.

Make time for love in your day
before missed moments
become missed years
of moving through life

rather than
blessing it
kissing it
finding delight in

the first crocus blooming in spring,

the cool kiss of fall's wind against your skin,

the way your teenage son towers over you,

the sound of your daughter's voice
singing a solo in your kitchen,

the scribbles on paper your toddler
presents to you as art,

your partner gently kissing your forehead.

Make time for love in your life
amidst the tasks that must be done,
amidst the worry, the bills to be paid,
soccer practice, piano lessons,
and deciding what to eat for dinner

to turn toward your beloved –
your child, partner, parent –
and without words of hurry
or thoughts of how they should be different

look at them with eyes of deep regard
lingering,
totally present,
and behold them.

Kindling Your Light Practice

Make time for love today and give someone your full presence and regard for five minutes. What shifts do you notice within you, the other person, and between the two of you?

## Keeping Love Simple

Let your love be simple.
Let it be enough –
a smile at a stranger out holiday shopping,
picking up trash on your way to work,
an encouraging hand on your son's shoulder,
a text to a friend who lost her dad.

Let these little moments of love be enough.

And extend yourself some grace.
You need it as much as anyone else needs it.

You are good.
I know TELLING you that
doesn't necessarily take away the doubt
or the drive for perfection.

So how about
starting to be gentle with yourself?

Tell that voice within you
that constantly tells you
you aren't good enough
or you aren't doing enough

that it's time she takes a rest.
She needs a break.
She's really trying to tell you that
she is tired of holding it all together.

So extend her some grace, too.
Let her off the hook.

You don't have to be good
or to believe you are good
to receive grace, tenderness,
and love.

Start with a simple act of kindness
toward yourself.

Open your eyes to see
the love around you.

Open your heart to see
your dear ones with new eyes.

Open your hands to receive
mercy and grace.

Let that be enough for one day.

## Kindling Your Light Reflection

Make a list of "little moments of love" that are possible for you to initiate, soak up, and enjoy – little moments of love for yourself and little moments of love for others.

## The Choice to Love

What would it be like
to hold nothing back, and to love
with your full heart?
To forget about perfection
and let go of expectations that
keep you tasting disappointment
each day?

This being human thing is messy.
Old habits wind and twist around
our throats, squeezing down
the heart's expression of love
until our jaws become tight,
we hunch over our hearts,
and hope dwindles down to
barely a flame.

Yet we are beings who can
wake up in any moment and
make a different choice.
It can be messy and imperfect.
We can stumble over our words
and yet we can still risk
unclenching our jaws,

straightening our spines
so that
our shoulders fortify the
back of the heart and
create an expansiveness
across the chest.

Let that heart of yours speak and
move you to take action that is
rooted in risking love.
Because your time here is
too precious for holding back.
Freedom is here now
in your choice
to love.

Kindling Your Light Reflection

Today, I am going to risk choosing love by:

## Loved as You Are

You are unique.
There's only one you.
Do I tell you that I love you enough?
Enough so that you remember
the truth of who you are on days when
the world isn't kind?
I don't love you for what you do,
what kind of success you have in life,
how well you do on an exam or in the game.
I love you for who you are,
as you are.

Let that sink in for a moment.

You are loved as you are,
for just being inherently you.

Today, carry that with you.
You are loved as you are.
You don't need to do anything to
earn my love.

You are loved.
You are cherished.
Always.

Kindling Your Light Practice

Tell someone today that you love them as they are. What do you notice when you express this kind of love? How does the person respond? What do you notice in the energy between the two of you? What do you notice happening within your body and heart?

## Bath Time

I am in the tub with my four-month-old son
holding his plump, new body in my lap
enjoying our leisurely exchange of
smiles and laughs
as I wash his back and under his chin,
behind his ears and between his toes,

when suddenly
it hits me
someday, hopefully a long time from now,
I will be gone

and there will come a time
when my son will be an old man
too frail to bathe himself
and someone else will need to hold
his fragile, old body,
wash his back and under his chin,
behind his ears and between his toes,
and I will not
be
there
to make sure they are kind to my son.

I am overcome with the primal panic
of a mother who cannot protect her child.
A grief I've never known before
grips my ribs and turns my stomach.
I am softly crying now – my tears mixing
with our warm bath water
as my son still smiles and giggles
and I continue to bathe him.

I breathe in deeply and then finally
let go
of that breath.
After a few moments I say to the grief,

"Yes, that is right, I will not
be
there."

I send out a prayer
to the nurse's aide or hospice worker,
my son's wife or grown child,
asking them to watch me now

as I gently rub a sweet lather
with a soft cloth and patient hands
over my son's trusting, vulnerable body.

And I pray that they can sense
how this now old man
was once so lovingly bathed

and they will wash his back and under his chin,
behind his ears and between his toes

with the tenderness of a new mother.

Kindling Your Light Practice

When you are out in the world, imagine that every single person had a parent who looked at them with love as a newborn and wanted them to be safe, happy, healthy, and live with ease in an often harsh world.

## The Invitation to be Held

For the mom who labored for hours
to birth her stillborn son

For the dad who was by her side feeling helpless,
wiping the sweat from her brow

For the person who wakes up each morning
with an ache of loneliness in her heart

For the single woman in her thirties
whose triumphs don't get recognized by our culture

For the husband who wants his wife to be happy,
to know he cares for her but often doesn't have the words,
and carries a heart full of unnamed shame

For the mom who feels responsible for everything,
and holds it all, yet can't ask for help

For the person who binges and purges

For the person who cuts

For the undocumented teenage boy
crossing the border with the help of a coyote
who will sell him tomorrow night

For the high school girl being bullied
not with physical threats, but threats of "not belonging"
that fly under the radar of school officials

For the Syrian refugees who flee war and death,
only to find rejection and death

For the elderly woman who sits in the nursing home
hoping her grandchildren will visit her today

For the elderly man who longs for reconciliation with his son
but doesn't know how to say, "I'm sorry"

For the child who wants to be held and noticed
but whose parents are too busy and full of their own hurts
to put down their phones...

May the world hear your cries.

May the world pause to see you, really see you
and remember that you matter.

May your griefs – named and unnamed –
seen and unseen –
be held tenderly, with spaciousness,
with no sense of hurrying,

in your own hands cupped around your cheeks,
in the hands of the Beloved who is holding you,
holding it all,
and in the hands of someone,
dear God, someone
in flesh and bones, who pauses long enough
to see you are hurting and what you are holding,
to feel your ache and respond with hands open
to hold you.

May you feel the warmth and compassion
of at least one companion who accompanies you,
offers you a cup of water, a nourishing meal,
a presence that says, "I see you. I am here."

May you know a true sense of safety –
the safety of a mother fiercely protecting and
providing for her children –
in your home, your school, your country,
and foreign lands.

May you have the spaciousness, the sacred space,
to grieve and moan with the sounds stuck under your ribs,
again and again, letting your cries be your prayers
that shake the world awake.

May you feel the full exhale that comes from
being seen, held, and acknowledged by one person,
millions of people, a nation, our world,
opening our ears to hear you, our eyes to see you,
our arms to hold you, our homes to nourish you.

May the world wake up today
to see you and respond with compassion.

### Kindling Your Light Practice

When you are out in the world today and someone bothers or frustrates you, make it your practice to pause for a moment, put your hand on your heart, soften your body and judgment, and remember that every single person desires the same thing as you – to be safe; to have access to high-quality healthcare, housing, and education; to be loved; to matter; and to belong. You might whisper to yourself a lovingkindness prayer such as: *May you be safe. May you be happy. May you be healthy. May you live with ease.* Then notice what shifts within you because of this pause and prayer.

## Go Gently

Go gently into your day.
Before you jump out of bed
and brace yourself to meet the world again,
pause and feel your breath.
Gently allow your hands to instinctually offer comfort
to the places on your body that have
already started to fill with tension –
a gentle hand on the knot in your belly,
a soothing palm cupping your clenched jaw.
Acknowledge what is here – the pleasant and unpleasant –
with the kindness and patience of a wise grandmother
listening to her grandchildren.
Whisper to all the parts within you, "I am with you."

Go gently as you dress,
eat your breakfast and greet your dear ones.
Slow it all down.
Welcome a soft smile to your face.
Soften the muscles around your eyes.
Let the love within you
pour warm light into
your conversations.

Go gently as you depart.
Linger just for a moment
to let your departing touch be gentle,
a sacred embrace to warm the hearts of those you hold
in this moment.

Go gently as you go about your day
so you pause before you pick up the usual worries
like a permanent backpack with heavy stones
that have made your shoulders ache
and fold in on your heart.
Go gently and offer your shoulders reprieve
with an expansive stretch and a gentle massage.

Go gently as everyone returns home,
greeting your dear ones with delight in your eyes.

Go gently into the demands of the evening –
from soccer practice to violin lessons –
slowing way down once again.
Turning off the phone and letting go
of the need to check email one more time.
And let yourself just be there,
resting, watching,
breathing.

Go gently as the day comes to an end
forgiving – yourself and each other.
Softening the harsh judgments.
Ending the day as you began –
feeling the comfort and warmth of your hand
on your heart and belly,

feeling yourself being breathed,
feeling the vast ocean of gentleness and compassion
smooth any harsh edges and
invite you now to
gently rest.

## Kindling Your Light Reflection

List all the ways you can go gently today and in this
season of your life – with yourself and with others.

# Evening

Peace

## It's Time for Quiet

That's enough work for one day, Love.
Put down the pen and paper.
Close the computer.
Put the phone on silent.
It's time to rest.
It's time to devote your
energy and time to
quiet.

Come back to YOU.
Slowly move your body
and stretch.
Like an ocean wave,
feel the vibrant inhale and
the cleansing exhale
of the breath
breathing
you.

Return to the
altar of your heart
and let me sit beside you –
breathing, resting,
dreaming
together.

Soak in the beauty
that you are,
now older, softer,
and yet even more
deeply sensual and
lovely.

Rest
in luscious surrender.
I'll fuel you and
guide you tomorrow.
Now – just
rest.

Kindling Your Light Practice

Give yourself a "Boundary Reset" – especially when it comes to sleep – by deciding on a time when you will turn off the screens, end your activities, put away the work, and get into bed. Try this for a few days and notice what a difference it makes to your wellbeing.

## Learning What is Good Enough

This is good enough for today.
I will not put more pressure on
these precious shoulders of mine
or prod myself to keep going.

This is good enough for today.

A long "to do" list still sits on the
kitchen island. I didn't make that
grocery list I planned on creating.
But, Jesus, this is good enough for
today.

I helped a friend make a decision
to stand for justice. I hugged my
children, fed the dog, planted a
row of tulips, wiped the crumbs
off the table and onto the floor
(which fed the dog again).
I saw a few clients – gave them
my best attention and focus.
I made bagel pizzas before
taking my children to soccer.

This is good enough for today.

It's time to know my limits,
call back my energy, and allow
myself time to replenish.
It's time to do the most
courageous act of loving myself
with exquisite regard,
loving my body – nourishing her
and regarding her as a temple
that has offered enough
for one day.

### Kindling Your Light Practice

Rest is a rebellious act of love. Practice telling yourself at
the end of the day, "This is good enough for today."

## Here All Along

Let go of
all grasping
and embrace
the One Love –
the Beloved –
who has
always been
right here
all along
inside
your
heart.

### Kindling Your Light Practice

Spend some time imagining a Source that has been here
all along inside your heart inviting you to let go and trust.

## Sacred Softening

My body knows,
has always known,
my way back to God.

I dance,

moving in slow sensual swirls
under the vastness of a moonlit night

swaying until stillness fills every cell
and there are no hard edges
striving, panting, thinking

only breath
and heart.

Empty now,
I open into spaciousness
becoming the brilliant Night Jewel
boldly, gently shimmering her soft light.

And I discover that
I have always been

resting

shining

in God's lap.

### Kindling Your Light Practice

Put on some soothing music and let yourself move slowly in sensual swirls. Let your body move organically. As you move, feel yourself letting go of the day and surrendering to divine spaciousness in your heart, mind, and body.

## Walking the Path of Beauty

I am walking the path of beauty.
Delight flows through me.
I love my body and treat it as a temple.
My heart is expansive
and my love radiates out into the world.
My feet step gently on the earth.

### Kindling Your Light Practice

Take five minutes before you go to bed and list the beauty you noticed in your day.

## Taking Refuge

I take refuge in you,
in the holy now,
the only moment
I have to live and choose.

I take refuge in you, my beloved,
your arms, your body,
your healing silence and embrace.

I take refuge in you, my Heart, My God,
beyond names or images,
my Holy Longing – my Home.

### Kindling Your Light Reflection

What do you take refuge in?

## An Unbound Heart

My heart knows no bounds.
My light radiates out into the world.
Everything is holy.
Everything
is prayer rising.

### Kindling Your Light Practice

Spend five minutes outside one evening looking up at the night sky, contemplating how big and vast the universe is and how you are made of the same stuff as the stars.

# The Poetry of Heaven

Some days
the way you smile at me
is like heaven singing poetry to my heart,
and I have enough sense
to stop what I am doing
and kiss this holy ground.

## Kindling Your Light Reflection

Whose smile is like poetry to your heart? As you bring an image of them into your heart, feel the nourishing, soothing energy of love and appreciation.

# When Only You Remain

What if I opened my heart so wide that
it included everyone and everything –
so wide that
I dissolved
and only
God
remained?

## Kindling Your Light Practice

Practice cultivating quiet – even for two minutes a day.

## My One Desire

I look back now
and I see how all my efforts
all my trying, yearning,
reaching, searching
and

letting go

have been to be
more deeply aligned
with You.

All my desires
lead
to
just
One –

only
You.

I desire
only
to
embody
You
in every cell of me
so fully that

I am
no
longer

and

only
You
remain.

Kindling Your Light Reflection

What is one thing you can let go of and let the Divine fill
that place within you with Love and Light?

# Whispers in the Silence

There is a voice within me that
beckons me to draw closer to silence,
to hear the beating of my own heart,
and respond with the utmost of regard
for what she whispers
in the silence.

## Kindling Your Light Reflection

What is that Sacred Voice within you whispering to you
when you are quiet?

# A Woman's Peace in Mid-Life

The older I get,
the less I want,
the less I look for approval,
the less I base my happiness on circumstances,
the less I try to change people,
the less I carry,

and the more I am aware of
the brevity of this life,
the more I trust in the Beloved's guidance,
the more I love my body,
and the more I find delight in the
smallest of everyday moments, like

my children curled up next to me on the sofa,
my breath on a crisp winter day,
warm socks,
tea with a dear friend,
my puppy snoring,
the golden pinks of the sun setting,

and in the quiet of the evening,
taking my husband's hand and saying,
"Come to bed, my Love."

Kindling Your Light Reflection

What simple pleasures and delights in life fill you with a sense of peace?

# Moments

Tonight I needed to sleep with the windows open,
to hear crickets and cicadas
to feel Fall arriving soon
to be reminded that
nothing is
permanent –

hot summer days
crickets, cicadas
emptiness, fullness
life, death
you, me.

Tonight I needed to sleep with the windows open
and feel God drawing me inward
into this moment with
my senses awake
my heart open

aware of how the little passing moments
of noticing, of being right here
watching my children's eyelashes flutter
taking a moment to taste my food

greeting my beloved at the end of the day
with kind eyes and gentle words

are the things that really matter.

Tonight I needed to sleep with the windows open
and feel the cool evening breeze kissing my warm skin
aware of how fleeting my life really is
and to embrace it fully, then

let it go.

### Kindling Your Light Practice

Let yourself be right here in this moment, remembering
that life is so very short and precious.

# Silence

I sit by the stream.
My breath, birds, water, and wind –
all sounds become one.

### Kindling Your Light Practice

Find a sacred place where you can be in silence every day. Maybe you need to create such a space in your home that's just for you. Maybe you look for a sanctuary outside in nature near your home that you can visit on a daily basis.

## The Way Home

I am quiet now
listening to my heart beat.
My breath leads me home.

### Kindling Your Light Practice

Put your hand on your heart and feel the breath flowing through you. Recall the moments from today of love and connection. Recall the times you chose to love – yourself and others. For the times you feel like you weren't patient or kind, put your hand on your heart and whisper a prayer of forgiveness. Then open your mind and heart to see the beauty, light, and love within you.

# Conclusion

## Resting in Her

In meditation this evening,
I laid down on the floor
and I cradled my head in my hands –
cupping my head ever so gently
as though I were holding a newborn.

Slowly,
I touched the back of my head,
sides of my head,
and forehead.

The image of my mother
holding my head as a newborn came to me.
I sensed how she must have
cradled my head in her hands
ever so gently and lovingly so many times.
I imagined how my newborn body would
have rested in her hands.
Surrendering completely.
Trusting completely.

I imagine
the Great Mother holds us like this
in every moment
inviting us to experience such tenderness
so we can rest in Her –
safely in Her arms.

A few years ago, I had a powerful dream that shifted the inner landscape of my whole nervous system. I was going through a time of feeling alone and anxious. This dream was like honey for my soul, welcoming me back into the deeper current of sacred trust beneath the surface waters of my fears and anxieties. I'd like to share it with you.

In my dream. an angel came to me. She told me that she was *my* angel. She said to me, *"I want to show you what happens when your life here ends."*

She went on. She said, *"You see, I am with you throughout your life. When you are about to cross over to the next life, I take your hand and I place it in the hand of this new angel. This new angel is with you in death and beyond."*

She introduced me to this angel. Then she showed me how she would have my hand in hers, take the hand of the new angel, and slowly place my hand in the new angel's hand while she slowly took her hand away. *"You see, there is never even a micro-second that you are alone. There is never a moment when your hand isn't in one of ours. You are never alone – in life or death."*

In the very first few moments when I woke up, I felt such a complete sense of peace. All worry and fear were gone. The usual tight constriction in my belly was gone. The anxiety in my chest was gone. Every muscle, organ, tissue, and synapse were relaxed. Within me, I felt a deep trust. I laid there for a moment, memorizing the landscape of my body receiving this experience.

Never alone. Not even for a micro-second. In life or death.

I felt the presence of my ancestors and their prayers caressing me. I felt the resilience of my ancestors – their hopes and devotion – fueling me, kindling my light.

I can't remember what happened later that day; I am sure the familiar anxiety returned. But since that dream and that embodied experience of such trust and peace, when the waves of worry and anxiety come as they do in our human experience, I can sense a deeper current underneath it all steadying me, reminding me, carrying me, cradling me, whispering to me, *"You are never alone."*

Now, when the surface waters of anxiety and fear rise up, I recall that dream. As I do, my body remembers the experience of true peace and trust. *"You can rest, Lisa,"* I hear from within me.

Rest. Remember you are held. Remember you are never alone. Remember you are loved.

Just as my newborn body trusted and rested in my mother's arms, the Great Mother calls me – again and again – to rest and remember.

This sacred "rest and remember" kindles the light within me. It enables me to listen to the Divine within me and honor what I hear. I can feel my ancestors calling me to rise with soul courage to let my light shine, to embody the sacred wildness of their prayers, and to share my medicine with others.

The Great Mother calls to you, too: rest and remember.

Maybe there are fears, anxieties, and worries swirling within you, speaking lies to you about who you are and who you are not. Maybe there are times you have felt alone. Maybe somewhere along the way, you lost that sense of trust in the Beloved. Maybe you have become harsh, bitter, and weary.

A current of Great Love runs deeper than your fears, anxieties, and worries. It cradles you. It flows within you. Always. Hear the invitation of the Great Mother calling you back into Flow. Hear Her through the noise of daily life to rest and remember:

*Rest now, child, and remember: You are never alone. Never.*

*Rest now, child, and remember: You are held. Always.*

*Rest now, child, and remember: You are loved. Completely.*

*Rest and remember.*

Rest is a powerful medicine. When you give yourself permission to rest, you more easily remember the ancient truth within you: You have a light to shine, a wildness to embody, and a medicine to share. You sense how the Great Mother and your ancestors call you to rise with their courage in your soul, to let your magnificent light shine, to embody the wildness of their prayers for you, and to share with others the medicine only you have.

May you know – deep in your bones – that the Great Mother holds you like a precious newborn in every moment, inviting you to feel Her love and tenderness so you can rest in Her – safely in Her arms. Always.

# Other Works by Lisa McCrohan

### Gems of Delight

*seasonal inspirations for moms to heal the hurry and embrace what is sacred*

Heal the hurry. Journey from busyness to pausing, harshness to compassion, and disconnection to sacred connection. It's time to revolutionize the everyday life of moms. We live, parent, work, and love in an increasingly busy, harsh, and disconnected culture. *Gems of Delight* invites us to slow down, connect with compassion to our own hearts and our dear ones, and live our everyday lives according to what is most sacred to us.

Lisa McCrohan offers moms a way to heal the hurry, be a compassionate presence in our families, and let our light shine. Through her poetry, conversations with God, and soulful reflections, Lisa shows us that connection heals us, compassion saves us, and surrendering and slowing down nourish us. Following the rhythms of the seasons, *Gems of Delight* offers short, prayerful inspirations that are perfect to pick up at any time of the year to feel nourished and inspired.

# About the Author

Lisa McCrohan, MA, LCSW-C, SEP, is a Somatic Experiencing Psychotherapist, Integrative Coach, and spiritual author and poet. Her life's work is about creating a more compassionate world through mindfulness, compassion, and sacred embodiment. She lives in Maryland with her husband, two children, and their dog, Sherlock, with the mountains outside their back door.

Photo credit:
Sarah Burns Photography

*If this book moved you,*
*please consider writing a review on Amazon or*
*Goodreads. Reviews are valuable ways to encourage*
*others to read the book and support*
*an independent author.*
*I deeply appreciate your kindness and support*
*of the mission to inspire a more compassionate world.*

**Visit the author at LisaMcCrohan.com**

Made in the USA
Monee, IL
26 April 2022

95353950R00113